Be Prepared

Creating Peace of Mind for You and Your Loved Ones

Jacquelyn R. Campbell, CPA, CFP®, PFS

Be Prepared

Independently Published

Copyright © 2023, Jacquelyn R. Campbell, CPA, CFP®, PFS

Published in the United States of America

151109-00268.3.3

ISBN: 9798394907685

Jacquelyn R. Campbell is a Registered Investment Advisor. Advisory services offered through Market Guard, a SEC Registered Investment Advisory firm.

No parts of this publication may be reproduced without correct attribution to the author of this book.

Here's What's Inside...

Introduction 1

Chapter One
Why Are More People Not Prepared When They Are Faced with an Emergency? 4

Chapter Two
Creating Peace of Mind for You and Your Loved Ones 6

Chapter Three
Critical Area #3: The Key Components to Include in Your *My When File*™ 9

Chapter Four
The Mistakes to Avoid When Creating Your *My When File*™ 20

Chapter Five
Your *My When File*™ Works for Many Different Personality Types 24

Chapter Six
How to Be Prepared and Create Peace of Mind for Your Loved Ones 27

Chapter Seven
***My When File*™ – 3 Step Process** 30

Here's How to Create Peace of Mind for You and Your Loved Ones 32

In memory of my Dad, Jack Yates and in honor of my Mom, Linda Yates
- thank you for making me feel loved and important.

Introduction

As a Certified Public Accountant and a Certified Financial Planner™, I have worked with many families regarding their loved ones' final tax returns and their entire estate process. In over 30 years of working with clients, when the unthinkable happens, I have observed many things which were done correctly and have also seen firsthand the added stress and burden on the family if prior planning had not been completed.

However, it was not until my own personal experience with the illness and untimely death of my Dad that I realized that I had not even helped the ones that I loved the most get all their financial affairs organized and in order. In the last 30 days of his life in the hospital, I was thinking about my thinking differently and realized that my Mom was the one in the family who knew everything. She was the CFO of the family, so she knew every document they possessed, where they were located, what insurance they had, where their income came from, what their expenses were and all the details about how they ran their lives. Dad, on the other hand, would not have had a clue where any document was. He would have been completely lost.

The realization that I was not alone and many people have no idea what their family's financial picture really is, made me stop and take notice.

The day a nurse came into his hospital room and declared, "This room is in dire straits. They need assistance with anything they ask." Those are words I'll never forget. That was a career-defining moment for me - I knew I wanted to write a book helping others put their affairs in order. Because words are often not enough, I want to help others so they do not have to go through the added stress and strain of not knowing where important documents are in advance. I set out to develop a system for my loved ones and clients to help them prepare for the inevitable emergency, whether it was an accident or, ultimately, death.

I count it a privilege to now help others by taking what I have learned about the math of financial advice and the journey of grief. My goal is to inspire you to design your *My When File*™, your plan, your operating system around yourself, your financial life and your wishes for those you love while allowing them to keep their conscience as you tell them what you want in your own life's playbook.

I hope it provides the clarity, confidence and direction needed to leave the legacy you want and encourages you to take the time to gather your important documents so you can create lasting added peace of mind for those you leave behind.

Enjoy the book!

Cheers to Being Prepared!

Jacquelyn R. Campbell

Chapter One
Why Are More People Not Prepared When They Are Faced with an Emergency?

One of the biggest reasons people are not prepared when they are faced with an emergency is the misconception that their time will never come. It is always in the distant future. Many people do not want to deal with discussions around death or disability. This is the reason many people put off doing estate planning. The reality is not if it will happen; it is a matter of when it will happen. I have found that most families spend more time planning a vacation than organizing their important documents and working on their retirement plans.

When something happens, and you have not prepared ahead of time, it is much more difficult for your loved ones. By handling some of the financial aspects and having a plan written out in advance, your loved ones are given a key piece of the puzzle, which makes it much easier for them.

While they are dealing with all the emotions and the grief, it makes that one aspect a little bit easier.

Chapter Two

Creating Peace of Mind for You and Your Loved Ones

I am a big proponent of the 3 P's: Prior Planning Pays.

One of my favorite statements that brings context to the meaning of this mantra is that *Clarity in what you want for the future brings clarity to your present.* No one plans to have an accident or to become disabled, get sick or go in the hospital, but these things do happen. These folders serve as a procedure manual of how your life operates and what to do if you're not here. You have your vital information there: contacts for your nearest relatives, who to call, your tax advisor, your CPA, your attorney, your financial advisor, and even a copy of your official documents. You might think someone can find this information, but in an emergency where time is of the essence, you do not want to take the chance.

The younger you start a personal file, the easier it will be to maintain and edit as your family grows, as well as your assets and net worth.

Let someone you trust know the location of your file, including important documents such as your security card, passport, birth and marriage certificates, legal documents and other official documents. You may not keep your originals with this information, but you can document where they are located.

Technology was supposed to simplify our lives. However, with technology, our lives have actually become more complex. Many businesses are 'paperless' or 'less paper', and most individuals have a combination and no consistency. We now store our files and records on a tablet, laptop, cell phone and paper. The challenge is that neither method of storing records is complete, and without the location of the information and the passwords, it will be difficult to follow. Photographs are a perfect example.

The bottom line is we do not have a procedure manual for our personal lives. Business owners have more complex situations and are even more at risk if critical information is not written and no succession plan is in place.

Most people are looking for clarity, confidence and direction in all parts of their lives. Peace of mind is what most of us are searching for. Documenting your financial life provides a better road map for your loved ones. Any time that you have clarity, confidence and direction, peace of mind will follow.

Benefits of creating your *My When File*™:

- o Personal Operation Manual
- o Less Stress for Loved Ones
- o Save time and money on legal and professional

Chapter Three
Critical Area #3:
The Key Components to Include in Your *My When File™*

Password Lists

One of the most important things to include in their vital personal records is a password list. This is a current list of your online, cell phone, tablet and computer passwords. This allows you to pass on the keys to your digital life in your absence, including social media. A cell phone is a perfect example of why passwords are very important. For some carriers, with your password, someone would be able to actually cancel your contract and save the estate quite a bit of money.

Some of the passwords may include:
- Email Accounts
- Online Banking
- Home Wireless
- Cell Phone Company
- Online Apple ID
- Social Media Accounts

o IRS Personal Identity Protection PIN and other governmental organizations

Emergency Contact Information

List important contacts to be notified or professionals who are key for data/information or who need to be notified when necessary.

Nearest Relatives such as children, close relatives, close friends, trusted neighbors or parents.

Important Contacts including
- o Financial Advisor
- o Tax Advisor/CPA
- o Attorney
- o Personal Representative
- o Power of Attorney (valid during lifetime only)
- o Trustee
- o Employer/work contact

Vital Personal Records

Official Documentation such as:
- o SS card
- o Passport

- Birth Certificate
- Marriage Certificate and any pre-or post-marital agreement
- Divorce Certificates/Agreement
- Military Discharge Records
- Adoption Records

Legal Documents

Another important component of your records is copies of your legal documents. These include your assets and liabilities, all of your financial account information, and details about your insurance policies. There are several things everyone should have once they turn 18, such as a power of attorney and a medical directive (a living will or healthcare surrogate). For anyone other than the individual to access medical information, you must have some sort of legal authorization. Otherwise, they may not give you all the information that you may need if your loved one is in the emergency room, for example. Adults should also have a last will and testament, and possibly a living trust agreement prepared by an attorney in their current state of residency to make sure there are not any other unforeseen legal issues.

Financial Account Information

Your financial account information must be documented. This can be a list of your assets: lists of all your bank account numbers and where they are. We are often working backward to verify what was on the tax return, and it seems that we spend a lot of time auditing to make sure we know where the funds are deposited. Also include a list of your investment accounts, retirement accounts and real estate.

Other information to include:
- o Personal Safe location and combination
- o Safety Deposit Box, bank location and key
- o Passwords – online accounts, your phone, tablet and for your computer

Insurance Policies

Typically to place a claim with insurance, you must have the policy information and sometimes even the original policy. When dealing with life insurance, you must have that information and actually file the claim; it will not be disbursed automatically. The same procedure applies to disability insurance and long-term care insurance. By having everything in one place, you know what type of coverage you do have: cancer policies, homeowner's insurance and even auto insurance. You can be prepared in case of emergencies by simply gathering a record of everything together.

Examples include:
- Life Insurance policy
- Disability Insurance policy
- Long-term Care Insurance policy
- Homeowner's/Renter's Insurance Coverage
- Auto Insurance Policy
- Health Insurance Card/Information – Medical & Dental
- Prescription Card/Information Umbrella Policy

Health Records

Have a list of your current medications, any allergies that you may have, and even your immunization records and diet restrictions that you might have. Include the contact information for your primary physician and if you have any other specialists. These are all important pieces of a puzzle in emergency situations.

Pet Information

Make sure you also list your veterinary contact and important medical information about your pets, such as the location of their prescriptions. Include any schedule that you may have for their medications and when they need the next medication. That is something that my mom had listed on a calendar, so it was very easy to follow, but I had no idea where she actually had the medication. Include anything to help keep everything going if you are not available.

Personal Property

It is important to list your personal assets and where they are located, such as your auto title and information and the title, home deeds, real estate, jewelry, and your home inventory. A great option is to record a video of your home inventory to have on hand for any homeowner's insurance if you ever need to make a claim.

One of my favorite discussions with the next generation is all the stuff in the house or out of the house handled. Imagine three or four siblings trying to sort out jewelry, collections, furniture, artwork, automobiles, family heirlooms, photo albums, motor coaches, Harley Davidsons, and on and on. I think this is worth a section of its own in detail.

List specific bequests such as your diamond rings and your jewelry: where do you want those to go? These notations are typically kept with your last will and testament so that they can be properly executed under the law of the state you reside in.

Long-Term Care Plan

If you want to have a plan for Long Term Care, address it now. Otherwise, you are waiting for someone else to make those decisions if the need arises. There are many options for planning to cover the costs of home health care, assisted living care and skilled nursing care. If you have a preference, please include it in your *My When File*™. By addressing this before a need arises, you help those you love by telling them your preferences and paying for the appropriate levels of care. Also, list any insurance policies or assets you have earmarked and would like to use to pay for these services.

Final Requests

This includes instructions after you pass, such as any prepaid burial details, the location of your burial, what kind of music you want to have played, and any non-profit donations that you might request in lieu of flowers or personal notes to loved ones.

My mother-in-law left personal notes to her children and grandchildren. This was a warming thing to give to her loved ones, in her handwriting, after she passed away.

One example of where the parents left in their will to their children how much they loved them and they hoped that they would be really good to each other, and to remember that they had worked really hard all their lives, and they did not want them to squander the inheritance that they had left to them. This showed the importance emphasized of those details for them to share with their family.

Those are the major elements of what should be included in your *My When File*™. We want to have all this information available so that when someone is in need, you have done all that you can to help.

I have some clients that actually tell their neighbors where this information is in case something happens; if their car breaks down and they have to take care of their pets or let their children know. It is a good thing to have that procedure manual for when the time comes.

With technology, our lives have become more complicated. Many businesses and most individuals have a combination of paper and virtual records, with no consistency in how they store their documentation. We have some of our financial and personal life in various digital formats, and without the key information, there is no trail for our loved ones to follow in case of emergency.

Years ago, everything was on paper, so they typically had nicely organized files. For each bank account, you knew where assets were held. They probably kept every statement sequentially for many years. It was a paper trail to actually go in and figure out what was going on in their personal lives. But now, with information sometimes on paper and sometimes digital, how do you know if somebody has paid their mortgage, or does it come out automatically? What action needs to be taken?

What I have seen with clients is that they do not tell their family members or their loved ones all of this information. There may be bank accounts that are not found for many months after someone passes away, or there could be more than one safety deposit box. If your name is not on it until you actually get the legal authorization to handle the estate or the trust, you are blocked from taking action, and there may be something in there that you might need to keep everything functioning properly.

It is the same as with photographs. We have digital photos randomly throughout our computers, or maybe even more than one form of media or device, as well as old photo albums.

Recently when we moved, it was a realization for my family that we have photos all over the place. It was a good reminder to actually police those things up. Are the computers and the tablets being backed up? Is there a backup procedure in place? If not, what should you do?

For business owners, their issues are even more complicated because they not only have their personal issues to deal with, but they have their business life, and that is a whole other list of passwords and other contact information for the important CFO for the business - their attorney, their CPA, et cetera. If you do not already have a written procedure manual, that should be part of your succession plan. If you have things documented, then somebody can fulfill your role as needed and keep the business going.

Chapter Four
The Mistakes to Avoid When Creating Your *My When File*™

One of the mistakes I see is not notifying your trusted advisor or your loved ones about the location of your file. You have created the documentation for someone to make their life easier, and regardless of it, you can have everything well documented. If no one knows where to find it, it is next to useless.

The next mistake I see is not making sure it is up to date. They need to make sure they review it and update it at least annually. We try to review that with our clients, at least during the first part of the year when we are preparing their tax returns, so that we can make sure that everything is up-to-date and accurate.

I have clients that every year bring me updated information for their trusted contacts in case of emergency so that if something happens to them, at least I know. They tell me ahead of time, "These are my children, this is my brother or sister, and this is my attorney, and so if something happens to me, please reach out to these people."

We have secure online access for our clients, and many of them give us copies of their estate documents so that they can have access to them over the internet when they are traveling, which can be very critical in an emergency.

Many clients work with an attorney to prepare the legal documents and designate beneficiaries for all of their investments. However, this is only one part of the puzzle. Often trusts are created and legally established, but they are not properly funded. The assets are not legally titled in the name of the trust, which can often cost duplicate work and more money after death or disability.

For example, if you have a minor child or grandchild, you may want to have a trust set up. Otherwise, depending on your state law, the courts will make a decision for someone who is either incapacitated or underage. If you do not have everything titled properly, with the trust being the name of the account or the owner of that account, it will have to go through legal proceedings called probate and actually be distributed into the trust. The bottom line is to try to keep the costs as low as possible and make sure that your plan is being followed as you would expect.

Most tax and financial advisors only focus on their areas of expertise and do not double-check the details of the ownership of your assets and how the estate plan will or will not work when the time comes. Many tax preparers simply work on the historical information because when you prepare a tax return, it is based on the prior year's activity, and they do not really look forward to "what if" scenarios. When we do a tax return for someone, we always look at several things: what is the income reported to IRS? What is the ownership of the account? Was it in just the taxpayer's name, or was it jointly held with the spouse? Is there a POD, Pay on Death beneficiary or TOD, Transfer on Death beneficiary on the account, or is it titled in the trust?

Sometimes, a person completely restates their trust because their marriage changed, or their family becomes a blended family with each spouse having children from a former marriage. In these situations, they often will completely restate a trust document, but they do not destroy or take all the assets out of the old trust. So when someone passes away, you end up with multiple trusts, complicating matters.

Chapter Five
Your *My When File™* Works for Many Different Personality Types

While many are organized in their own way, I find that most have scattered and inconsistent recordkeeping, beneficiaries which are not up to date and don't match their wishes, passwords not complete, and they simply are not 'ready' for an emergency.

A perfect example would be an engineer I met. As you know, engineers are generally very, very detailed. They look at how everything works, and they are very methodical with their thinking, so they usually have everything documented; they cannot have peace with themselves until they know they have done everything they possibly can to make it easier for their loved ones. On the other hand, there are many examples with clients where nothing was done: no estate plan, no last will and testament, and no living will.

If you are over age 18, a living will and Durable Power of Attorney, POA, are the most important legal documents. The POA is one of the most powerful legal documents that you can actually have during your lifetime. Many do not even tell their loved ones that they have power of attorney. A power of attorney is only active during someone's lifetime, so at their death, a power of attorney is revoked. This document can give someone the authority to buy assets, sell assets, and make legal transactions; completely act as if you are that person, depending on state law. When someone is under 18, they are considered a minor, so the parents would already have that power of attorney under state law. It is so simple and very, very inexpensive to prepare.

Many people do not want to deal with the issue of their demise and subsequently do nothing to prepare. They do not look at the ownership of their assets or business; they do not have long-term care insurance, disability insurance, or even life insurance.

Life insurance is typically used to replace your income for your family and to cover your debts and expenses in your absence. If you are a high-income earner and you do not have any income replacement for your beneficiaries, your loved ones will suffer financially. With a little help, it becomes a lot easier than it sounds, and it is truly a loving gift to leave your loved ones – prepared to move forward with their lives in the best possible financial shape.

Chapter Six
How to Be Prepared and Create Peace of Mind for Your Loved Ones

There are a lot of moving parts in creating a procedure manual, especially when you talk about wills, estate plans, and insurance policies. If someone is interested in having our team help them, we work with them to make sure that they are prepared when an emergency happens.

The first step is a consultation in our office to discuss how we can assist them in completing and organizing the necessary information for their loved ones, and we offer three levels of assistance. We can assist with the purchase of *My When File*™, which is a notebook that outlines exactly what they need to help them organize and summarize the information. They can buy this product and answer questions that will help them in the case of an emergency so that someone will be able to have all the contact information, insurance information, and bank account information at their fingertips.

Most people hesitate to actually take that first step, so we have created fill-in-the-blank forms for them to make it a little bit easier for them. We can consult and review their organized information and provide some recommendations for improvement. We can help them sort through their documentation and summarize everything for them, and then meet annually and update everything.

An important question for most is whether this information is kept safe? We do not want the wrong person to get ahold of all of our bank account information, so how did you address that?

If you give this book to someone, you want to make sure that it is someone that you trust, whether it is a close neighbor or a family member, or even one of your personal advisors. With today's technology, we make everything available online, offering a secure way for them to store that documentation.

Most people have someone they trust or have a letter of instructions for them of where they have it hidden. This is a lot of confidential information, so you certainly would not have this key information lying on your coffee table. Giving directions to one of your personal advisors about where the location of that book is, when the time comes, is part of the process.

Putting something like this together can be done in a couple of hours, or it may be more involved. It depends on your personal situation and how many assets and accounts you have, and how organized you are. I estimate about 20 /25 hours to collect everything together, have the accurate copies and get everything started.

It is time well spent because if you just had everything in disarray, it would be stressful versus spending the time upfront. Have everything organized; it is a gift showing you cared enough to want to make it as stress-free for them as possible.

I think it is a timely reminder that you should not put it off. If you wait until you have a health crisis, you will possibly not have the capacity to put it together. Do it while you are healthy and young, and then it is just a matter of updating it. If you have questions, call our office at **352-683-7365**, or send us an email at **info@mycampbellandco.com**.

Chapter Seven
My When File™ – 3 Step Process

As a Natural Problem Solver, I created a 3 Step Process and a template for what I call a *My When File*™. This is a place to compile all of your important information and documents to make it easy to find "When" the inevitable happens.

1. By creating your own personal *My When File*™, you are able to provide many important details about your personal and financial life in a convenient, secure location.

2. Notify your trust advisor or loved ones about your personal operation manual, *My When File*™.

3. It should be reviewed and updated at least annually. Creating and updating your file regularly will keep everything current, convenient and accurate for your loved ones in case of emergency and 'when' the time comes.

Create → Notify → Monitor

Here's How to Create Peace of Mind for You and Your Loved Ones

If you were in a car accident or had a serious health crisis today, would your loved ones be prepared to handle your affairs? If not, it's time now to take action! This is especially true if you are in the 'Red Zone' of retirement. When a loved one passes on without their financial affairs being in order, the hardship and stress for the family can be quite staggering. The time-consuming part is not knowing what information is needed and where to store the information so that everyone will know where to find it.

That's where we come in. We help people just like you with a step-by-step process for organizing and storing all of your important documents.

These are the three options we offer:

Option 1: Do it yourself - It's time to clean up your messes. Give your loved ones peace of mind by investing some time to get organized by buying our storage system and filling out your very own *My When File*™ at **mycampbellandco.com/my-when-file/.com**

Option 2: Prepare a draft and ask for help and improvements - Once you receive your *My When File*™, organize as much information as possible, and we will review and provide recommendations for improvement. There may be areas where you are not fully protected, and we can help you fill those gaps.

Option 3: Ask for help - We assist you in organizing your important information and work with you annually to make sure everything is updated and current.

Now you can create clarity, confidence, direction and peace of mind for you and your loved ones in just a few easy steps with the checklist, forms and organization system. We encourage you to provide a copy of your *My When File*™ to your family, financial professional, accountant, attorney and executor annually. This will ensure that everyone will have documentation of your life and know exactly where to find it.

If you'd like us to help, just send an email to: **info@mycampbellandco.com,** and we will take it from there.

Made in the USA
Columbia, SC
19 December 2023